CONTENTS

1.	What are Curses?	1
2.	What kind of Curses are there?	7
3.	Past Life Curses	12
4.	Family Curses	20
5.	Present Life Curses	23
6.	Everyday Attachments	28
7.	Entities – from the Mild to the Demonic	34
8.	How do I know if I have a Curse?	39
9.	Psychic Protection	45
10.	Clearing your self	53
11.	Clearing your Home	59
12.	Clearing your workplace	65
13.	Other Ways to break Curses	70
14.	Creating Impenetrability	75
	About the Author	83

1
WHAT ARE CURSES?

Curses and spirit possession are older than white man's written history.

While the Christians would define a 'curse' as a malediction, I would simply call it a decision to direct harmful energy at another, using words and/or ritual, with a force of intensity behind the focus.

Anything that we send out with intensity will have an effect, which is why it's wise to follow the ancient tribal motto – 'whatever one sends out, one receives three-fold in return'.

A fellow intuitive, in a fit of pique 15 years ago, sent out a silent curse muttered under her breath towards someone who was creating harm, and broke both her own legs in the following week! For her, it was a profound lesson, as she told me that what she had envisioned for this man, was exactly what she received back, and more.

We can often become aware that we are cursed through a dream. It is a powerful spiritual practice to learn the symbology of our dreaming, develop a strong trust in our own intuition and learn how to act upon the dreams we are given. We know inside of ourselves that the dream is simply a roadmap, a movie that holds clues about the health and well-being of our outer world.

One dream I acted upon immediately was one in which I saw dark storm clouds, rolled up carpets and was visited by unwelcome intruders into my house. I woke up, cancelled my appointments for the morning and meditated until I discovered the identity of those sending dark and threatening energy towards me. Once I saw their faces in my inner vision, I could relax a little and plan my curse-lifting. For me, it's always helpful to know the identity of a curse-sender, as it means I can clearly visualize them and place them into the centre of my clearing ritual.

I baked a dish, adding protective herbs, conducted a waning (releasing) moon ritual and 20 hours later the curse had been lifted and I was free to progress. So, trust your dreams, and be responsible about the energy you carry inside and send outside.

When you feel rage or deep pain because of another, practice redirecting that intensity into a creative rather than a destructive form. Don't get mad, get happier – plan your future without this person around you, and use the force in you to travel up and clear out your heart space instead of clogging it with resentment or guilt. Smile, and confuse the enemy, so they say!

Anyone can deliver a curse, and traditionally, those sent via experienced shamans or psychics may have a greater effect. This is because, due to practice and experience, their concentration and ability to hold an affirmation or visualization may be sharper and more continuous than someone who doesn't meditate or 'journey' on a regular basis.

Traditionally, the shaman, sangoma (witchdoctor), medicine woman or man of the community would be the one to lift any Curse. Like the teachings of the church, the methods of development were not in the hands of the common people, for various secrecy or control reasons.

Each community shaman or priest would also have their own methods of releasement. So, while the clergy might perform their rituals with incense, chanting and in some cases, the beating of sticks, others – like some Native American shamans, would lie down next to the person in need of treatment and travel with their energy to the lower 'spirit' world to access healing.

Religions are the usual domain for energy clearing and protection in the Western world, and naturally the ritual of christening or baptism is a form of exorcism or curse-lifting.

Indeed, if you investigate the biblical references of Christianity for example, you'll find that Jesus commissioned his 12 disciples to 'heal the sick and cast out unclean spirits' (Luke: 9). Ministers today perform 'deliverance' on those carrying curses, or 'demons' – and every now and again, one reads in a newspaper that someone has gone too far in their method, with fatal consequences.

The list of famous curses abounds. Historically, there are many religious curses, including God's curse against Satan for tempting Adam and Eve, and Islam's Allah cursing Iblis for not bowing down before mankind.

Then there are the mythological curses, many of them involving a particularly unhappy ancient Greek, such as Hera the goddess of marriage who cursed the women who were seduced by her roving husband, Zeus.

There is debate as to whether the Ancient Egyptians used curses, but the possibility of the existence of Egyptian curses may be enough of an incentive for archaeologists and tourists to let sleeping dogs and Pharaohs lie in future.

In the USA, one of the most well-known curses was delivered to the US presidency by a Native American shaman in the 1800s. He cursed the existence of the white men in power and vowed that, starting with William Henry Harrison in 1840, the person elected every 20 years would die in office. This was true for Abraham Lincoln in 1860, Chester A Arthur in 1880, William McKinley in 1900, Warren Harding in 1920, FD Roosevelt in 1940 and JFK in 1960.

For some reason, it didn't affect Ronald Reagan in 1980, which might lead one to wonder whether a curse-lifter was recruited to erase the shamanic deliverance. What's interesting to add here is that his wife Nancy was interested in astrology and consulted on often. Forewarning of such a possibility may well have helped thwart the assassination attempt on her husband's life in 1981.

Another example of famous curses would be ones exchanged between two ceremonial dark magicians, Aleister Crowley and MacGregor Mathers.

The heaviest curse of all might be the one delivered by the Christian church to a priest they are excommunicating. It involves the reading of ancient and damning text that forever condemns the poor soul to hell, a bell is tolled and holy candles are inverted and extinguished.

Methods of cursing are as varied as creativity will permit – from traditional effigies used in parts of India, Africa, Egypt and Europe to the 'cursing stones' of Ireland; the Chinese ritual of leaving rice and pennies outside an opponent's door and the infamous 'elephant gun' in Africa - an 'imaginary' gun that can be directed across thousands of miles from a witchdoctor to his victim. There are no studies that can accurately estimate the number of victims who have died from curses, rather than from their own fear that leads to sudden death, but the thought is eerie, nevertheless.

Symptoms of curses could be symptoms for any imbalance of energy, really, so it can be a challenge to pinpoint the origin of the life-situation. They can range from a family history of accidents or diseases, healing not being received, a difficulty in moving ahead in one's life, ongoing financial or health problems, premature death, multiple miscarriages and so on.

By now, you might be feeling paranoid!

However, be assured that not many people nowadays understand the full extent of intensity required to send a potent curse. Those who work with energy know all too well the ramifications and don't go anywhere near this temptation either.

Not everything that may feel challenging in your life is incoming energy. Some of your life difficulties can be due to genetics, attitudes, internal judgements, resistance to letting go of old pain and the financial strain of living in today's modern world. Ideally, our focus throughout our life is to practice letting go, rather than accumulate, in all its forms. To hold the intention to have an impact upon the planet in loving, powerful and harmless ways is to be a powerful intuitive.

Hopefully, by following my methods, you can not only discern what's coming from yourself and what's not but learn how to let go of any old energy, so that you can move on and into the best of your life!

And letting go of curses ain't like Hollywood either. No banging doors, rushing wind, twisting heads, scared priests and lifting beds – not if you know your options. For the most part, curses can be lifted without any fuss at all – certainly the ordinary, everyday ones.

My techniques of curse-lifting in this book are not tied in with any religion, dogma or creed, and nor are they harmful in any way. If your first thought is to visualize scenes from 'The Exorcist', know that there are kinder, gentler yet firmer ways to remove unwilling spirit attachments and curses for good.

2

WHAT KIND OF CURSES ARE THERE?

While we can define the different types of curses around, it can be a challenge to work out what type of Curse you may be carrying within your energy, as – regardless of the type – most have the same effect. Your life force energy reduces, it becomes hard to attract powerful and prosperous events and people into your life, your health may suffer and you may generally feel tired, drained and heavy.

Family Curses are those curses which are launched against a family group. Usually these originate when a family is placed in a position of power and abuse it. These curses can often be traced through karmic astrological means, as a chart can reveal a series of cyclical events and tragedies that occur from generation to generation.

One such family that comes to mind might be The Kennedys.

In 1969, when Senator Edward Kennedy faced the collapse of his Presidential hopes after Chappaquiddick, he asked whether there was a curse on his family. Teddy Kennedy joins thousands who have pondered the same thought.

Here's a brief list of some of the family's troubles over the years:

- Joseph P Kennedy Jr, Joe's eldest son and his ambitious father's great hope for the American Presidency, is killed in a plane crash in 1944, aged 29.
- Kathleen Kennedy, Joe's second daughter, dies in a plane crash in 1948, aged twenty-eight.
- John F. Kennedy, 35th President of the US, is assassinated in Dallas in 1963, aged forty-six.
- John F. Kennedy's son, Patrick Bouvier Kennedy, born prematurely to the President and his wife in 1963, dies three months before his father's assassination.
- Robert F. (Bobby) Kennedy, Joe's third son, is assassinated in June 1968, aged forty-two.
- Edward M. (Ted) Kennedy, Joe's youngest son, drives a car off a bridge on Chappaquiddick Island in July 1969, after a party. His aide, Mary Jo Kopechne, is found dead in the submerged car. His political career has not survived the speculation surrounding the incident.
- Bobby Kennedy's son Joseph is involved in 1973 in a car accident which leaves a female passenger paralysed for life.
- Ted Kennedy's son, Edward Jr., has his right leg amputated in 1973 because of cancer.
- Bobby Kennedy's son David dies in 1984 of a drug overdose.
- Ted Kennedy's son Patrick is treated for cocaine addiction in 1986.
- Ted Kennedy's nephew, William Kennedy Smith, is acquitted of rape in 1991.

- Bobby Kennedy's son Michael is killed in a skiing accident in December 1997, aged thirty-nine.
- John F. Kennedy's only surviving son, JFK Jr., dies in a plane crash in July 1999 (exactly 30 years after Chappaquiddick), aged 38.

Set out this way, it's clear something energetic is afoot by the sheer scale of tragic events in this family's history – but take a breath as you begin to think back upon your own. Every family has repetitive behaviours and patterns, however, some of these are for good. Whilst you may inherit dysfunctional or tragic patterns, you may also have been granted some gifts and good fortune along the way.

There's also the 'Anniversary Syndrome' as some therapists call it, which can describe behaviour that may suddenly emerge when an individual reaches the precise age at which his or her predecessors themselves re-enacted an ancient misfortune. Again, this syndrome can be traced by deft astrologers.

Probably one of the easiest ways to offload a family curse is to open the Pandora's Box that tends to hold a family secret. Nothing is as potent as a family secret passed down from generation to generation and nursed in the darkness of silence for years. Secrets build up in terms of energy, which is why they are often become even harder to reveal with the passing of the years.

Heal the next generation if you have the courage, by clearing out your closet of dark secrets and learning how to speak them in a supportive and safe environment.

Choose a support group of strangers, a therapist you trust or a friend who will not judge you – and practice letting the darkness out and the light back in. Light dilutes the power of secrecy and it's essential we clear them. Work from the basis that everybody you know holds a secret or two – so you are not alone. To let go of one requires you to make a choice of loving yourself more, opening to more in life and moving past the old shame or guilt that binds us to secrets. Shame and guilt are both 'learned' behaviours and are not natural emotions and the good news is – that anything we 'learn', we can unlearn.

Love and acceptance are your natural state. Ask any six-month-old baby!

Other types of curses include:

- ones you have received from past life encounters from other people
- ones you have placed upon yourself unwittingly in this present life or past lives, and
- the everyday attachments collected from passing energy as we live our lives within the 'aura' of humanity's 'collective unconscious'.

The 'collective unconscious' could be defined as the area beyond our auras in which we, as humans, collectively toss out our random thoughts of violence and pain. Now, imagine you choosing to have a swim in this sea of powerlessness, where we all dump our negative thoughts and limited affirmations about ourselves and others … much the same as swimming in a polluted river! Bacteria, like collective unconscious energy, are hard to see, but you begin to feel the effects within.

In addition to your own personal index of possible curses, you may need to also take your choice of geographical location into account. Some curses can be associated with tribal ground, graveyards and other power spots unknown to your culture or upbringing. For this reason, trust your intuition, always tread carefully and with honour and protection, should you be in a position to visit old tribal lands or sacred sites. Aldo, acknowledge the guardians of the land, remembering to thank their energy when you arrive and before you leave.

Wherever you live on the planet, there are also astrologers that can pinpoint specific places across the globe that are karmically and energetically beneficial for you to live in, or travel to.

It's also a wise idea to dowse a new home before you move in, and to cleanse and protect any living space you choose to inhabit, just in case there are any old hexes or curses lying around that the last resident forgot to take with them!

There are also energy curses that dwell near psychic doorways or energy portals that are invisible, for the most part to us. Because these are harder to tap into it, trust your intuition. If you are walking past an area, and you notice your body reacting – perhaps a tightening or contracting in your 'chi' area – the chakra just below your tummy button – then automatically surround yourself in brilliant light and ask for the protection of your guides.

Then, there are the curses used by traditional magicians and members of black magic covens, called 'egregors'. Anytime a group is involved in an energy focus, more power comes from it, whether it is a coven or a group of focused healers. Again, strong and grounded protection is your key to impenetrability!

3

PAST LIFE CURSES

Think back to when you last uttered a strong, intense thought about something – or someone. It could have been the last time you held your child and whispered into his or her ear, 'I'll always be with you', or murmured words to the love of your life, like 'I'll never love anyone the way I love you.'

It could've been yesterday – or a long time ago, depending on your life. Or perhaps you can only recall the way, Scarlett O'Hara, her fist in the air, vowed 'as God is my witness, I shall never go hungry again', in that classic movie 'Gone with the Wind'.

By the time you have read this chapter, you may think twice before you direct your intensity towards a vow, oath or promise – because, quite simply, whenever an affirmation, be it positive or 'negative' with intensity, it becomes an oath in our energy system, that is carried with us for not only years to come – but for lifetimes to come.

How many oaths, vows or promises have you uttered in your countless past lives that have brought you to this point?

How many intense decisions that have come from powerlessness or rage have you made in your current life?

We can carry unresolved blocked or frozen energy within us which remains until we either heal, rescind or officially withdraw our intensity from the vows made.

Once released, we can move forward again, open to loving more freely, growing our self-esteem, receiving prosperity again, forming bonds of friendship, speaking our truth and increasing our leadership potential.

Our body has its own truth and the longest memory of all. Only by tapping into our energy system can we begin to unpeel the wrapping that preserves hidden secrets that hold us back from happiness and health.

We place so much importance and emphasis on our minds, and revere academics and those with strong intellects – yet, the most limitless part of our self is our spirit, the part of us that remembers everything from numerous life times and events - and the body, as its protector, holds the spirit energy.

So, we must begin to listen to the *'bodymind'* – the mind that runs the body. Just as I believe that many physical conditions originate from stuck emotional energy, so we can discover – through various techniques and therapies like rebirthing, bioenergetics, connected breathing, hypnotherapy and deep tissue massage, to name a few – how to learn the language of the bodymind.

Once we tune into this, we can begin to become deeply aware of what our body is trying to tell us. Then, when we feel a contraction in the chakra just below the tummy button, home of 'chi' or 'lifeforce energy' we can immediately give yourselves a 'time out', have a work break, find a quiet place and tune in to discern what's happening. Usually, your first, intuitive impression will be the right answer. And, while your strong intellect/mind will start to analyse and question the response, practice going with the flow of the answer and choose to stay in the emotion, the feeling or with the body. If it requires you to cry, rage, speak something, own something, walk away, pound a cushion – then do it. You don't need to know why and how – just do what your body wants you to do, and you will feel the difference.

So, trapped within the bodymind, is trauma from this life and former lives. These decisions can prevent you from choosing to have a relationship, get healthy or rich or spiritual or be independent, almost as if the oath, vow or promises has become a protective mechanism against the possibility of future pain.

One client of mine came to see me about her fear of drowning. She was convinced that she would drown and had become exhausted at her rituals of avoiding bodies of water at all costs as a safety precaution. The truth was that she had already drowned in a previous life, and her energy carried the memory of that trauma.

Intensity stays with us.

Ask anyone who has experienced the loss of a loved one and they will be able to tap into their grief and pain, as if it were yesterday. Trauma can remain fresh within the bodymind, until we can do the work to let it go.

So – how do you know what oaths, vows and promises you might have made in a past life?

Have a look at the following list and see whether you resonate with any of these:

- a loss of identity, feelings of not belonging
- the need to stay at your post well beyond the need (such as to stay in a terrible marriage out of duty)
- a tendency to follow orders without question
- a feeling that you are constantly on your guard
- a constant questioning of your life purpose
- a tendency to caretake everyone else except yourself
- your self-worth comes from making others happy, even when it conflicts with your own needs
- a fear disguised as 'respect' of teachers and others in authoritarian positions
- a fear that you'll never acquire enough knowledge or qualifications
- a fear of expressing your truth
- focusing on a 'real' job instead of your passion to be an artist, for example
- a fear of being rejected for being imperfect
- a need to distance yourself from the world
- a feeling of being trapped within a body
- a strange inability to grow your wealth
- a fear of 'being discovered'
- while being great at helping others heal, you find you cannot heal yourself
- a tendency to avoid relationship, or going deeper within relationship
- an inability to fall in love and let go completely
- a fear of acting upon your own initiative or in personal power
- wanting to be separate from different cultures, religions or even the other gender.

These are just a few of the beliefs created by an experience in which a repetitive pattern has been created, due to an oath, vow or promise!

Major vows, oaths or promises we all have uttered in past lifetimes can include:

Religious and Spiritual Vows:

- Poverty: unable to be prosperous without feeling tremendous guilt
- Chastity: look at it this way - if you were married to God in a past life, why would on earth you be available to a partner in a relationship?
- Obedience: unable to use your personal power, but follow orders instead
- Silence: as you may have had to withhold sacred teachings and not reveal these under pain of death in a past life, today - as you cannot recall what's sacred and what's not, you now reveal nothing, or forget everything
- The Healer's Oath: an ancient ritual that forbade healers to partake of healing energy but to use it all for others, as it was considered to be limited in nature (although now we know this is incorrect).

Power Vows:

- Fear of Consequence: 'if I let me light shine too brightly, I will die.' Many women carry the memories of lifetimes within 'The Burning Times', the approximately 300-year period in history which over nine million women were said to have died. What if it happens again, your memory urges you, even though you may live in more peaceful times?

Wartime Vows:

- Death before Dishonour: this will have you stay in terrible relationships, threatening situations long after you should leave and continue to serve people who don't appreciate you.
- Weight-Holding: after a life as a victim of war, a decision to 'never go hungry again' has contributed to your ability to lose weight, even though you are in a different body in a time of peace.
- What's My Mission: you continually search for your mission, your purpose as if awaiting instructions.
- Got Money, No Money: currency slips easily through your hands, connected to a memory of earning money dishonourably in the past (and now you have no desire to live in this manner, so best to get rid of it quickly, just in case!)
- Revenge and Retribution: you will live in a state of vigilance and reactivity, often from the memory of witnessing loved ones slaughtered. These decisions are stored in the bodymind as 'fuel' to keep the vow alive until it can be 'fulfilled'.

I probably don't need to mention here that it's crucial for your health to release these. My own experience of releasing an ancient Celtic vow to despise all English men brought up feelings of grief and loss, with a thought that came in of 'who will I have to hate now?'

There are a host of other vows that happens in a variety of different lives, which I explore in my workshops regularly, but for now, I would consider these some of the most important. In the meantime, visit my website (lucybaker.net) to heal via my hypnotherapy journeys to other lives and release.

Another method is to do your own clearing.

To journal your impressions, first have an idea of which vows, oaths or promises are affecting you now – write them down, then find yourself a quiet space. Light a candle, make sure you are comfortable and move into relaxation, breathing deeply and getting a sense of your spirit energy becoming aware and strong, as your mind goes to sleep.

'If in any lifetime, I took vows or made oaths preventing me from ……………….I hereby rescind those vows for now and for all time. I now open myself to receiving the benefits of ……………… in this life and beyond.'

As you finish saying the words, breathe deeply and imagine a strong white light moving down through your crown chakra, down your spine and beyond, into the earth beneath you, anchoring in your rescinded affirmation. Begin to gather a sense of your guides, or a presence of warm healing green or rose energy surrounding you, and then imagine that you are sitting in the palm of a great hand – the loving hand of the Universal Energy, God, Goddess, Great Spirit – whatever name you place upon it. Breathe and feel the blocked energy begin to seep out along this central channel of light within you and out of your crown chakra. You may have noticed its colour leaving you.

Then close your crown chakra when the energy feels complete, when you feel no more vibration, lifting or movement – by imagining a flower closing down its petals, sealing in your energy, and sending a warm golden seal around your aura, protecting and rebalancing you.

This may clear some for you. Other, stronger ones will hide, which is why we all need an outside facilitator at times to draw them out of us. But, for now, try that.

It can be that easy. Then commit to focusing on your new openness, take some risks and start acting in ways that can affirm that you are now free of the past. Remember, whatever you focus on, grows!

4

FAMILY CURSES

Family curses, are those carried through the genealogy, affecting each generation with an affliction or tragedy – until the Curse can be acknowledged and broken.

Another example of a family curse is that of Sarah Winchester.

Sarah was born in the 1830s and married into money when she wed William Winchester, from an influential gun manufacturing family, inventors of the famous Winchester Rifle.

Four years later, they had a daughter who died six months later, a traumatic event that would set the course for an obsessive behaviour for years to come. This event also sparked the earliest thought that a family curse may have occurred. Sarah slipped into a deep depression and remained so until William's death 20 years later.

Upon her husband's passing, Sarah inherited $20 million plus half of the ownership in the Winchester Repeating Arms Company – all of which sadly brought her little comfort, having lost the two people she loved most in the world.

Still depressed, she sought the assistance of a medium who told Sarah that the family has been cursed by the spirits of all those killed by Winchester rifles. This rather irresponsible woman added that the spirits had taken Sarah's daughter and husband in revenge. Sarah's only solution, the medium said, was to buy a house and continuously extend and improve it. It also appears that the medium advised Sarah that should the construction end, Sarah would die as well.

Sarah purchased a house in San Jose in 1884, and immediately started using her $20 million fortune making various additions twenty-four hours a day, seven days a week, 365 days a year, for the next 38 years, only ending the day she died at the age of 85.

Today, she might have received a gentler diagnosis of obsessive-compulsive disorder, some intensive grief-counselling and therapy, perhaps. But back then, she was convinced it was indeed a curse and that she had work to do.

Her house had 160 rooms – including 40 bedrooms, 13 bathrooms, and 6 kitchens. There were also 47 fireplaces, many of which had flues that led to nowhere, as Sarah believed the spirits after her could enter and leave a house through the chimneys.

There were two ballrooms, and forty staircases, and more than 450 doorways. Of the forty staircases, many ended nowhere. It was a strange maze of confusion, increased by the additional presence of rooms with windows in floors, bedroom closets that opened to blank walls and one door that opened to an eight-foot drop into the garden.

No wonder the poor woman had no peace!

The exhausted Sarah died in 1922, at the age of 85, and was

buried alongside her husband and daughter. Her house, in its original form, is now listed as a National Historic Site.

The good news is that we can explain much of what we used to think of as curses, in terms of mental health disorders, medicinal reactions and science nowadays.

Have a look into your genealogy and discover whether there has been a line of misfortune or strange obsessive-compulsive behaviour.

Medical conditions can often be hereditary, but if other events are occurring alongside an affliction, then you may have cause to believe that there is a family curse alive and well along your ancestral line.

The good news, as soon as we can accept a truth, we can do the work required to let it go.

5

PRESENT LIFE CURSES

As mentioned, every time you utter a vow of intensity, the thought sticks – and it gathers energy every time you think of it. Eventually it will become a fully formed, determined block of energy that will ensure that you meet with success in terms of fulfilling the vow.

This is exactly why it's best to try to end all relationships on a karmically peaceful and harmless note. This means that, instead of leaving his phone on the international timeclock, sowing grass seeds around his apartment, cutting his ties in half and selling his Porsche for $10, you make your ending quick and harmless! The less energy you use in a break-up, the better.

The modern ritual of 'ghosting' – when someone simply drops out of contact and blocks another on social media – ensures your energy is intertwined with that person as an ongoing hindrance to your combined health! So, while it's convenient, it's also a little cowardly, dishonest and karma is served up once more unfortunately, so be clear and say what you need to say.

You will avoid the possibility of having any difficult person re-enter your next life to complete the contract the two of you set up when you were souls prior to incarnation.

Choosing to see each person in our lives as a teacher is the most powerful way to live. We learn something more about ourselves with each connection, and even more so with each challenging connection!

Who do you need to forgive and who do you need to complete with?

Unresolved relationships can often carry 'curse energy'. Luckily, it's never too late to heal the hurt. You can't energetically forgive anyone until you've worked through your rage, but you *can* begin to heal yourself with a decision to stop holding onto pain.

When we feel helpless or powerless, we want to lash out – it's only natural. Yet, if we were to see what that energy looks like, we might think again. What if we chose to take our rage, our hurt, our grief to another place – to a space where we could release it safely and effectively without harming anyone or ourselves?

Our responsibility then, is to be sure about what we send out – as it's possible to curse ourselves with intense and malicious intent.

Next time you are in a store and you see a young child having a tantrum, watch and learn. This is healthy anger management at its finest – you are seeing someone clear their feelings in a clean, not blaming, loud and healthy way. Remember, you used to be a child too, so somewhere in you is either the instinct or the memory of when you did this for yourself.

And, because it's in you – you can drag it up from the foggy recesses of your memory and do it again. You know how to do this! Isn't that great?

How life changes. Look at how your parents 'did' anger, then look at what you learned from them. Either you'll do it in a loud, out of control, head-on collision kind of way that can often be scary and violent – or you take it inside, and let it seep out like a silent and deadly snake in the grass, with a snide remark here, a malicious sentence there, designed to slowly destroy someone's self-esteem instead of the sudden intensity that goes with the loud version.

Both are dysfunctional, ineffective and awful. Anger turned inwards creates depression and women represent most of the depressed human beings on the planet right now. Depression lowers lifeforce energy, and with this, our ability to magnetize and attract good things into our life. So, you get smaller and smaller. Just think how much bigger and more joyful your energy could become if you took a risk and tried a whole new way of doing things.

If you're brave enough – or angry enough about how you do anger, then make the change. The best thing about anger is that it changes things – so use it now to make a new start in your life, find out where your nearest anger workshop is and learn some new behaviours.

The best thing about learning how to clear anger is that underneath it is passion. In fact, the feelings in the body as you express your rage are almost identical to the feelings your body has when you are in your passion – vibrating energy, breathing fast, raised energy levels, bubbly feelings – remember? So, as you let it out, you will get in touch with the good stuff again.

I learnt a great technique for this at a workshop in the bush of

Australia one sunny afternoon ten years ago. As luck would have, an ex-boyfriend was also present that day – and as time went on, I began to feel more and more tense, then angry until finally I had to walk out of the room, so focused was I on all the things he 'had done to me', etc. I was in 'victim mode' and I was livid!

One of the workshop team members offered to help me clear this blocked energy and led me outside. There, by a river lay a mattress. He handed me a baseball bat with a smile. I stood there, not knowing what he wanted me to do. All around me was peace and serenity, warm sun on my shoulders, blue sky above, the sound of cicadas, kangaroos contently nibbling at grass a hundred yards away and an emu munching just a few feet away, unconcerned with the turmoil raging within me. The team member looked at me.

'Go ahead and close your eyes, think of your feelings, let them build up then begin to hit the mattress with your bat as hard as you can, and open your mouth and let whatever words come out, whatever sounds come out. Just go for it.'

I closed my eyes, and did what he asked – and surprised myself with the amount of force I was putting into each swing of the bat, words beginning to spill out of my mouth, almost as if my bodymind took over and knew what to do. I shouted and screamed and raged and swore like a trooper, and beat the hell out of the obliging mattress again and again. My mother would've fainted.

Then, almost as quickly as it had begun, it was over.

I was aware of a sudden drop in intensity and a feeling of calmness spread through my body like warm caramel. As I took a breath, a feeling of self-consciousness came over me and I slowly opened my eyes and glanced apologetically at the man watching me, but relaxed as I saw his loving expression of acceptance.

Then I glanced over to see how far the animals had fled to – and got the shock of my life. They had not moved one inch. The emu was still munching a few feet away from me, and beyond it the kangaroos.

That's when it hit me – that to them, angry energy was just that – energy, like wind, like sun, like music or breath. I turned and smiled at them. Anger didn't have to be scary anymore for me.

So anytime I feel upset by anyone or anything in my life, I know what to do. I even have a punching bag outside especially for me. My family knows that when I am outside, and I am shouting, mom's fine, and that it's just anger work. It's not about them anymore, it's about me, and I'm working through it. Loud is OK, anger is OK so long as it's expressed safely, and then it's OK to get back into joy and clarity again. The feeling of release and lightness is the best thing of all.

If we can all take self-responsibility for the energy we send out, trust your intuition, keep your energy pristine and make a lifetime affirmation to be loving, harmless and utterly powerful – you become truly protected and curse-proof.

6

EVERYDAY ATTACHMENTS

Attachments, entities…it all sounds very dramatic, doesn't it?

In fact, it's part of life and our bodies are used to it. Just as our physical skin flakes off as it dies, and a new layer grows underneath, so our energy is a moving, vibrating instrument that attracts and repels other moving, vibrating energy around us.

Have a think about this. On an auric level, the first layer of our auras that lies closest to our physical body is a bright, white thin band of energy and the most easily seen of all the layers. Now, inside of that band are millions of tiny particles of debris from our physical bodies, such as mucous and skin! Also, did you know that the reason we have colours within our auras is because the chakras spin the colour out from the centre of our bodies?

So, what we need to remember is that we are shedding ourselves constantly, and what we do inside of ourselves has a direct effect on what we can attract to us, energetically, psychically, physically and emotionally.

Look at the room around you. It used to be a thoughtform in someone's mind, in someone's inner vision. Now it's a reality.

Now imagine taking a trip through the mall and tuning into other people's energy as you pass them. Then imagine how you might feel, after walking the whole distance from one entrance to the exit on the other side, after you have focused in on everybody.

Exhausted, perhaps – drained and scattered?

This is one exercise you might not want to try, but its effect, if you are not fully protected will be a great burden on your energy.

'Attachments' are like heavy, sticky, dark clumps of energy, with varying weight and intention. They are common to many folks and usually enter when your tiredness and unprotected energy field creates a portal, a door through which other people's heavier energy can pass. The most popular doorways in our body energy would be through the crown chakra, the brow chakra or third eye and the back of the neck. Other secondary ones would be through the pelvic chakra, just below the tummy button and the solar plexus.

Coincidentally, these are also the hotspots – the top favourite places – that other people's energy can 'cord' or attach themselves to you on a long-term basis.

Attachments originate from three main sources.

   1. People you know:

A lovelorn admirer, a possessive ex-boyfriend, a needy friend, narcissistic parent or a controlling teacher. An example of a controlling teacher could either be a minister who encourages co-dependence and advises you to listen to his teachings alone, or a Reiki master without integrity who attunes you and enters your auric energy at the same time. Yes – it happens, and it can make the rest of us Reiki masters look bad. One student of a particular character in my town went to have her Reiki attunement with him and that night, awoke to find his energy in bed with her! So, it pays to be cautious always.

1. Proximity to people

From working in a group environment, going to a late-night party, having unruly neighbours or just by living in a busy city, it's easy to collect a range of scattered and emotionally-laden energy. If you're a city girl, escape to the sea or countryside regularly as it will automatically recharge and rejuvenate your energy.

I live in Canberra, a small Australian city of around 400,000 people which has a more grounded and clearer energy to that of Sydney, a city of millions, about three hours' drive away. Energetically, this means that, unless the Sydneysiders are well protected and relaxed of mind, life is more aligned to progress in smaller populations.

This is not just my opinion. Aboriginal people describe Canberra as the 'heart chakra of Australia' and its most transformative city. So, choose where you want to live, as much as your circumstances will allow – or commit to finding the grounded areas within your city.

Attachments, therefore, are a fact of life – as there will always be the chance of a stranger walking past you with energy to send out.

The good energy sent towards you, you don't mind, like the smile, the happy magnetic connections – but it's the heavier stuff we need to talk about. Someone could walk past in his own world, seething with rage over an incident, plotting revenge and you may well end up with a doseful, if your own psychic boundaries are not pristine.

Another thought to ponder is that, in addition to humans in the shopping mall, there are also the attachments sent from earthbound spirit, such as those who live in your house. But fear not, we'll deal with all of them!

1. Through an Abrupt Event:

The third way for you to gain an attachment comes through the portal that occurs when sudden and abrupt change happens, like a car accident or an incident of abuse. In that moment, your energy is at its most vulnerable and at that moment of impact, an energy will enter your being. Imagine someone who has just had surgery for a life-threatening disease. Sometimes they appear to be different people or show an aspect of their personality that you might not have seen before.

This type of attachment, I believe, happens frequently with organ donor operations. New body parts, still carrying another person's energy, are added or inserted to another person's body. Medically miraculous, but energetically dangerous – unless you know how to cleanse the new addition.

The organ donation issue can often be a source of dilemma for many people who work within energy. I, for instance, carry an organ donation card, primarily because of my belief in reincarnation and that the body is just a temporary shell that carries the soul in for a single lifetime. However, I also know that, if I do not resolve to take all of my soul energy with me when I pass over, I will leave some behind in my organs for another to unintentionally inherit. It's a bit like leaving your garbage in a house you are vacating!

So, an end of life-time ritual, a simple meditation in which you instruct your guides to remove all your soul energy from the physical body at the time of passing, is a good idea to put into action. You can do this on the next full moon or in your next meditation, if you like. Lock it in, just like making a Will.

Making plans won't bring the event closer, but it will safeguard your future. And, if you do this, you can carry your organ donation card and know that you are making a difference out there in the world, one that is of harmlessness and love rather than the opposite!

Now, what happens in that sudden, abrupt traumatic event then, is that your vulnerability creates an immediate portal for an attachment to zoom in, like a nurse rushing to an emergency room.

Initially, the intention of this incoming energy is to *protect you*. Strange, but in my years of experience, I have found this to be true. However, the longer it stays inside you, the more complacent, difficult and controlling it becomes, and it resists change fiercely.

This means that when you instinctively try to break free of its hold, it will create struggle in your life until you surrender to its control again. Only by specific and focused work can you release such an attachment.

It sounds the exact opposite of everything you saw in 'The Exorcist' or read about in Christian exorcisms, doesn't it?

And so much more empathic and healing.

7

ENTITIES – FROM THE MILD TO THE DEMONIC

There are more serious attachments called 'entities' – and can range from mild cases to demonic energies that have created their own persona, even down to their own name. And, while you can easily remove the milder entities, you may need help on the outside of you, with the darker elements.

This is where someone like me, a curse-lifter, comes in. Using specific trick questions and communication, I will determine what type of entity it is, when it entered and assist it in going towards the Light. It's a thorough process that requires excellent boundaries, heightened protection and patience on my part, and it works beautifully. Often the person it has attached itself to, sleeps through the entire session, which takes between 30 minutes to two hours, depending on its size and strength.

As entities can range in power, the intervention of a third party such a good metaphysical or psycho-spiritual hypnotherapist is the best approach. Without access to these, it's also worthy to remember that the Light is always stronger than the dark, no matter the situation. Your strong, disciplined and well-protected focus is the key to health.

Entities are a huge distraction for anyone who wants to be happier and purposeful.

I had a call one day from a woman in her forties whose life had 'stopped'. She could no longer summon the energy to get up in the morning, her relationship was crumbling around her and every time she applied for a job, she failed to win the position. Her daily thoughts were scattered and, try as she might, every time she attempted to re-evaluate her path, work out priorities or decide to move forward, her mind would fog over, and she'd develop an overwhelming urge to sleep.

In frustration, she came to see me the following day and immediately fell into the deep relaxation I guided her into. There, within a safe and nurturing space, I let her mind and physical body rest, while I focused my attention upon the part of her energy that was 'wise spirit', the part that remembered everything and understood the reasons for any blockages or challenges in her life.

During my discussion with this part of her, it became clear that she had a lodger, an alien presence that lived within her energy and had done so for many years. I gently coaxed this presence to enter a conversation with me, and reluctantly it finally came to the surface.

Often entities do not want to be disturbed as they like to remain invisible. Once spotted by someone like me, they will instantly descend into a torrent of abuse, and make it clear they do not wish to move, change or leave this person they are inhabiting.

A good psycho-spiritual hypnotherapist will gain the trust of this grouchy energy and ask it about its job, how long it has been living within the client and whether it's happy.

The answers are usually the same. The job of an entity is to control the person, to make it hard for them to gain ground and move ahead. Originally though, when an entity first enters a person, it is usually in a split second of trauma – like a car accident, surgery or a moment of abuse and its mission, to honestly protect the sufferer from any more harm.

When they enter a living person, usually an entity behaves in a helpful manner and acts like a good Samaritan, granting strength. However, once it gets comfortable, it develops its own ego and wishes to control its person. It also likes to feel needed, so of course, its biggest threat is when its host becomes too self-empowered and self-reliant.

The only obvious way to prevent this is for an entity to naturally curb the person's energy, try to keep them 'small' and limited, and to induce sickness or depression as an incentive to not move ahead.

When I asked the entity whether it was happy, it had the standard answer – of course not, because the host was difficult to deal with – always wanting to grow beyond its influence! In a way, entities are a bit like controlling parents who find it hard to deal with a teenager who is becoming his own person.

Life is all about letting go – and even entities must come to terms with this.

I then suggested that, as this person was obviously so unappreciative of the entity's commitment and dedication to the task at hand, that it leave, go 'home' and have a nice holiday. As usual, this thought is quite new and a little scary for an entity to contemplate – as they never recall where they were before entering their human. In my client's case, this entity had been with her for 15 years.

Through the trust developed between us at this point, I can then gradually – as if I am speaking to a child full of fear of the unknown – encourage the entity to notice the presence of guides in the room and have the entity choose one to go towards, take the hand of and be guided to the Light. This moment of release is the most honouring part of the process for me, the room is often filled with a radiant light and the feeling in the room is quite moving as a recognition of true safety seeps into the consciousness of the lost, dark one.

Now, as I sat there and watched, the room gradually emptying of guide presence, accompanied by the entity – my client suddenly sat straight up.

'Oh!' she exclaimed and looked at me. 'What happened? I feel as if I've lost a leg!'

I nodded my head and gently asked her to close her eyes and breathe again as I brought her out of her hypnotic state in a grounded way, making sure to close her crown chakra before she came back into her physical body, for safety and protection.

The feeling one feels after the removal of a curse or an entity is an emptiness, almost as if an actual body part has been removed. Such is the weight and moulding to the host's energy that an attachment has. However, this is a 'good' emptiness – and my client was now able to fill that space inside with Light instead.

The next day, she called me to say that she had had a call about a job offer and that she was feeling very clear. Her life was continuing onwards again.

To prevent another entity moving in, she then needed to remain positive, protected and to choose uplifting, limitless thoughts about herself and life.

In the midst of the darkest of darkness, always look for the spark of Light.

Light is always present, no matter how small. The process was delivered with caring and gentle firmness, not at all like the shaming and menace that accompanies religious exorcisms. In my view, that attitude only results in a defiant attachment that results in a far more lengthy and torturous session. No, the real, spiritual method is honouring and empathic – and the results are a lot more effective.

For the most malignant and serious entities, such as demonic energy, it's crucial for you to seek out experienced curse-lifters who have worked on this level before. Thankfully, most entities and attachment are like the one my client had just released.

Filling our homes and our heart with love is a key to enormous self-protection. What we put out, we get back.

8

HOW DO I KNOW IF I HAVE A CURSE?

How do I know I have a Curse?

When bad luck or tragedy is recurring, the first action you must consider taking is to cleanse yourself and your space, examine your thoughts and take some self –responsibility for your own personal growth. When you can clear your energy of limited and negative or old, unserving patterns – you are on the road to impenetrable psychic protection.

On the psychic level, you also gather the discipline to keep your energy pristine and unavailable for outside attack. Commit to having an aura that only love and light may attract, almost as if you are inside one of those old mirror balls we all used to see so much of in the seventies!

Here are some of the most common symptoms of attachment or entity possession:

- low energy levels
- character shifts or mood swings
- a feeling of 'something coming over you'
- sudden, reckless or impulsive behaviour
- inability to remember things
- poor concentration
- paranoia about food and drink as if poisoned
- hearing an inner voice speaking to you
- sudden onset of depression or anxiety
- sudden physical conditions that seem inexplicable
- inability move forwards in life
- feeling drained and depressed
- noticing strange odours
- a feeling of heaviness, as if there is a weight upon you
- inability to think clearly
- inability to make positive change happen in your life
- failure to win jobs or develop healthy relationships
- nightmares and insomnia
- having a sense of something around you that is not part of your own energy
- constant thoughts of someone who dislikes you
- dreams that are full of violent or threatening imagery
- physical conditions that seem to appear for no reason
- sudden, irrational fears

Now, many of these symptoms could be attributed to mental health and everyday non-spiritual conditions, so I would encourage you to first seek medical and professional advice before assuming you have a curse or attachment.

. . .

There is a fine line between what we know and are only just beginning to consider on a psychiatric level and I know the idea of spirit releasement will be a common practice in contemporary health at some stage.

However, sometimes the mind can play tricks. The more one thinks about the possibility of a curse, the more one can believe it to be true, as in the case of Salem, the setting for a tragic series of events caused by ignorance, fear and paranoia.

On a cold dark Massachusetts winter day in January 1692, eight young girls became suddenly ill, beginning with 9-year-old Elizabeth Parris, the daughter of Reverend Samuel Parris, as well as his niece, 11-year-old Abigail Williams. Theirs was a strange sickness, its symptoms including delirium, violent convulsions, incomprehensible speech, trance-like states, and odd skin sensations.

The conclusion reached by the villagers was unanimous and dramatic – someone in their town was laying curses upon the innocent!

The first to be accused was the Reverend's slave Tituba, followed by Sarah Good and Sarah Osburn, two elderly women considered of ill repute. In short, over 150 'witches' were arrested, with 20 put to death and a further five who died in jail.

On October 29, by order of Massachusetts Governor Sir William Phips, the Salem witch trials officially ended, and with that the trance ended. A strange air of bewilderment reigned over the village with accusers at a loss to explain their own actions.

Humans love drama – and to believe this was a Curse is heady drama indeed. However, the reality of science is beginning to take over the historical tale – and it began with the discovery of a common grain fungus.

Fast-forward to the 1970s.

When Linda Caporael, a university student, began to research the Salem witch trials for her thesis, she had little idea that her work would change a story. As her investigative work progressed, Linda noticed a link between the strange symptoms reported by Salem's accusers and the hallucinogenic effects of drugs like LSD. LSD is a derivative of ergot, a fungus that affects rye grain.

Ergot thrives in warm, damp, rainy springs and summers, exact conditions that were present in 1691. The rye crop, a staple grain for the villagers was consumed in the winter of 1691-1692, shortly before the 'bewitched' symptoms were reported. That rye, Linda determined, could easily have been contaminated by ergot. The summer of 1692, however, was dry a condition in which ergot did not thrive which, 'coincidentally' also explains the abrupt end of the strange behaviour witnessed.

Toxicologists now know that eating ergot-contaminated food can lead to a convulsive disorder characterized by violent muscle spasms, vomiting, delusions, hallucinations, crawling sensations on the skin, and a host of other symptoms - all of which are present in the records of the Salem witchcraft trials.

So, notice what you do with Fear! Too much of it and it will become the drama that runs your life.

In one curse-lifting session, contaminated plants didn't come into the case of an elderly Greek lady who came to see me one day, accompanied by her niece as she was unable to speak English.

Her situation seemed dire. She was experiencing depression, exhaustion, nightmares and had an intense fear of being poisoned. She had lost weight and her paranoia had increased to the point that she couldn't bring herself to eat any food at all, but drank only water.

After moving her into a relaxed hypnotic state, I began to ask pointed questions directed at her bodymind to discover whether she had an ancestral or cultural curse or an entity existing within her energy.

There are several trick questions one asks of an entity – and sure enough, she had one. This dark clump of energy intent on destroying its host turned out to be connected to an ancestor who had received the original curse during his lifetime and had obligingly and unknowingly carried it beyond his generation to affect all those who came after him.

Through the niece acting as translator for all my words, this devoutly religious lady with no experience of entities, was able to release the entity, visualize its departure and feel its release from her body. By the time the session was over, she carried a lightness around her again, her skin tone had cleared and her energy was high, yet calm and grounded. She called me a few days later to thank me and let me know that she was ravenously eating again and that all was well.

So, while the existence of curses and entities are quite real, our fears can often compound problems or, in the case of Salem, create new myths.

The word 'FEAR' is an acronym for 'F*** Everything And Run'! We run inwards, shut down progress and come from the memory bank of the past that urges us to not move forward in case something 'bad' will happen to us again.

What if we chose to change this belief of ours – and in doing so, rename the acronym to 'False Evidence Appearing Real'? Then, trust and move forward.

Your purpose is usually in the direction of Fear. Maybe you are ready to find it, now you are more aware and a whole lot braver.

9

PSYCHIC PROTECTION

I believe we are all intuitive creatures.

It takes us only seven seconds to decide whether we like someone upon meeting them, according to a recent Harvard university study. There are no chosen few when it comes to accessing our psychic abilities, and it has only been in modern times that humans dismissed the notion of a sixth sense.

Many famous leaders have employed a combination of mental power and intuition, such as Einstein and Branson, in order to make a difference.

In life, it's always a powerful choice to develop your psychic abilities in order to be guided onwards on your path.

Intuition is like a muscle: the more you develop it, the stronger it gets. Intuition will save your life, warn you of dangerous future events, help you access solutions through dreamwork and meditation and also advise you when greater protection on an energetic level is required.

To protect yourself psychically, the more that you engage all six of your senses in a protective process, the stronger the protection. The rest is mental repetition and maintaining an attitude that is grateful, positive and as judgement-free as possible in order to keep your energy field pristine, safe and strong.

I always advise my students to imagine that they are astronauts on an earthplane chockfull of unconscious collective energy which, to my intuitive senses looks and feels like swirling polluted mud that lies beyond our energy fields. Just as you'd wear a protective suit as a sewage worker, so it's best to treat outside energy the same way.

You are already intuitive. The use of your sixth sense is a very ancient memory imprinted into your genes, from many ancestors across the world.

Get to know more about energy, and practice your visualization skills. Surround your car, your home, your loved ones with colours and become familiar with creating a force field around you that prevents anything except love and light entering.

The magic of psychic protection works with the energy of people. However, the moment we become blasé or complacent about our force fields of protection, the Universes will send you a warning.

This is happened to me 12 years ago.

It was at a time that I felt very poor, life was a struggle and bills felt quite overwhelming. I was a single mum and trying to make ends meet, so when I got the call from a man who wanted a reading, I leapt at the chance to make some money – despite a feeling of uneasiness.

His name was John. He gave me his address, we fixed a time and within an hour, I was on my way. I had arrived at his home late morning on a weekday when the kids were at school ... a run-down house in an area of my city I'd never liked.

There is a term called 'sympathetic resonance' in which we energetically connect to other people or communities that mirror our own level of awareness and intent. For me John's house felt alien ... there was something heavy and unseen about it. Still, I focused on the electricity bill I would be able to pay after this session.

Against my intuition, I knocked on the door.

A smiling young man opened the door to show me inside. As I walked into the living room, I noticed my energy within my body, especially my stomach area, begin to change in the most alarming way - in a jumpy, edgy, butterflies sort of way. Before the words were formed inside my head, my bodymind knew *something was wrong.*

There, in the lounge in front of me, sat three people, dressed in black, on a couch looking at me in silence. In his own chair, sat the man I had come to read for - legs sprawling out in front of him towards a small table, hair down to his shoulders, aged in his forties, with a curling smile.

Now, I have nothing against the colour 'black', as it's been used in powerful, healing and cleansing rituals for hundreds of years, and can be a positive colour. However, when it is used within a deeply dark or negative context, the effects can be overpowering. We all have shadow-selves, but here I was, in a room with a man who was so comfortable in his shadow that he was willing to take as much advantage of it as possible.

At this point, a sudden and horrifying insight into my

consciousness. *I was in the house of a leader of a black magic coven.* This was going to be a battle between dark and light. I instinctively knew that this was a necessary test for me. I had become dangerously complacent around my protection, having worked within the field since 1972. When we get complacent, we let our defences down.

This would be the very last time in my life, that I would ever disrespect the importance and power of energetic protection.

I looked and sounded casual as I took out my tarot cards and sat down. I used to play poker, so I know how to put on a 'game' face! As I shuffled the cards, John and his three followers watched me, looking for signs of vulnerability. I strengthened my 'disco' mirror ball I use as the exterior wall around my aura and could feel the reflection of the man's shadow totem animal, a black wolf, prowling around me trying to find a way in. It didn't succeed and only bumped its nose on the shield. Throughout my time there, I could feel those people trying to gauge me and my level of fear. It was like a test between dark and light.

From the moment I had entered their energy, my totem animal inside me - a large and powerful lion was gone and, in its place, a rabbit cowered, trembling.

I was struck with one clear certainty.

I was going to die.

My children were at school, no-one knew where I was, and I was going to die. They would not find my body … perhaps it would be buried under the floorboards and life would go on, but no one would ever know. I would not be leaving this house intact, I was convinced of it.

The energy around me pressed in on me, around me, black, sticky and murky. I felt as if I were attempting to walk upright through molasses. I took a breath and began the reading.

It was quite clear to me. I had a choice to succumb or to strengthen. In the darkest of darkness, there is always that pinpoint of light, remember.

As we faced each other across the table we were two warriors of different energies. I chose my position, faced him with a direct stare and began his reading - one of ambition, greed and involving the takeovers of other, weaker people.

Inwardly, I told the rabbit to go and fetch my Lion - an animal symbolizing my innate strength, groundedness and power. The totem who has lived within me ever since I began my psychic journey at the age of eight.

The rabbit disappeared. I began to silently recite 'The Lord's Prayer', an ancient chant of highly protective energy, and started visualizing myself surrounded with rose-coloured energy emanating from my heart, the energy of Love. Golden energy streamed into the top of my head, through my crown chakra, illuminating me from the inside and spreading beyond my physical body to an exterior cocoon of rose. Around this, a thick ring of impenetrable, powerful white energy sealed me from outside influences.

I began to feel as if I could breathe again, my lungs felt lighter, my airways clearer. All around me, the energy began to gradually shift. The light expanded as I grew energetically stronger and bigger.

I answered John's questions as briefly and as unhelpfully as possible, focusing on my inner activity, picturing myself extending my powerful light outwards, outwards, into their dark space – just as they had intruded upon mine.

Then, an interesting side-effect began to happen.

The three previously motionless people on the couch began to shift uncomfortably on the cushions, and the energy of John began to soften and dissolve under my gaze. The lion was back, and the Light was controlling the space now.

Gradually, my energy expanded along with the light, my body relaxing and, while I still completed my reading in record time, I felt that the danger of me forever losing myself in the black, sticky tar of their energy, was gone.

I finished the reading, packed up my cards, declined the offer of coffee from a now docile and small energy called John, and drove away.

As I drove, I prayed. I thanked my team in spirit for their protection and the valuable gift of the lesson. Even though I had been doing this metaphysical work safely and well for nearly 30 years, it was obvious to see how complacency can taint any one of us. Never again would I tread so carelessly in my work and my Lion has never left me since.

Rather than learn the hard way as I did by having an abrupt event like this happen to you, you can develop your trust in your intuition and hold gratitude for your protection by creating rituals that enhance the power in objects you are drawn to. These might include crystals, natural objects or jewellery that you've bought in shops or inherited from family.

One of my favourite methods is to bury a newly acquired object in the earth for four days and dig it up on the fifth day. Another way is place it outside in the sunshine for four continuous days.

There are others, such as salt and full moon water immersion, so choose one that feels right to you. Then what you do is hold it and program it with your own energetic intentions.

To restore your own energy, if you are feeling drained, down or depressed, here's a lovely, simple restorative meditation that has always worked wonders for me.

I imagine all the negative fears and thoughts that are surrounding me as tangled wool. Then I step away from them, placing them all into a bag that I toss either outside or into the corner of the room. Now it's time to concentrate on me and who I really am, away from the crushing weight of insignificant, human insecurity and mind games. I breathe in deeply, and as I breathe out, I can allow myself to do one of several things, depending upon where I am - scream loudly, shout or scream silently with open mouth and body straining. I reserve my really loud screaming or roaring for the car when I'm driving!

Then I take another breath and begin to imagine my body begin to be covered up with a beautiful, shiny golden foil. I also imagine I see a team of loving angels do this for me, wrapping me up as tenderly as a mother would do to her infant, the golden energy making me feel warm and secure.

I then imagine this foil begin to puff up, with each breath of mine - until I am encased within this golden balloon of shining love. Gold is one of the ultimate protective colours in the spirit world. I finally fill the inside of my bubble with rainbow light that, as I breathe it in, feels soothing and powerful.

Mmmm! I must tell you, this works extremely well after an argument or before a job interview. Use it and let me know what you think.

Follow your intuition, as I've said before, and notice the signals that come to you through dreams and thoughts or feelings, that may alert you to a need for greater protection. The next step is to not allow the mind to procrastinate a necessary action. Receive it, then do it.

Also, be open to developing your intuitive senses through the act of dreaming, whether these dreams happen during the day or night. I take my dreams very seriously, and indeed, only recall the ones I need to take heed from or act upon. Notice the emotions you have upon awakening and try not to move any part of your body until you have gathered two or three images from your last dream that you can bring into your waking moments and interpret intuitively. Jot these reflections down immediately. Then, make some time in your busy day to focus within an intuitive or quiet space. No dream book can interpret your own dream – they can only guide you.

At the end of the day, you need to follow your own wisdom. However, please remain a student and learn more skills from teachers you are drawn to.

10

CLEARING YOUR SELF

The single most important discipline in psychic development, moving through personal challenges and simply evolving as a human being is how to keep yourself grounded during the process. Without clear boundaries and the knowledge that you are always in control, you may feel as if you are driving a fast car down a hill with no brakes!

Also, after any type of energetic work, my students learn how to close their chakras down - to imagine each of the seven major chakra as flowers, and visualize the petals, one by one, closing down for a period of time. I begin at the crown chakra and continue down the body to the base chakra, and this final one I leave partially open, to help me reconnect to the earth.

I cannot tell you how many meditative groups and teachers there are who are not aware of the importance of closing the crown chakra, much like the closing of a sturdy and well insulated bank vault door. Often at the beginning of a class, they encourage their students to open but fail to have them leave re-insulated and safe. If you are within such a group, ensure that you do your own level of high protection and, if you are a group leader from now on consider creating a safer learning space for your students.

While there are many great books out there on chakras, here's a brief introduction to them in simple terms: When you think of a chakra, an energy centre within the body, an easy way to picture it is as a clothes spin-dryer, with its little round window at the front.

Whilst we all have around 67 of these power spots in the body, often we will focus on the seven major ones, that live in a semi-straight line from the crown of the head and along the spine in seven fixed points. In my experience, these seven often will turn either clockwise or anticlockwise at slower or faster rates of movement, retaining power on an energy level and spinning out their colours into the aura. They draw up the energy from the earth and draw down the universal energy from above our heads and feed us with it in the form of vitality, passion, joy and healing.

Some cultures believe that for nine days of every month, our chakras change direction. For some practitioners, they will note these days as particularly intense or magnetic. Using either a pendulum or dowsers, it's easy to monitor the direction of your chakras daily. To see how I work with dowsers on an energetic level, visit my *pastorlucybaker* YouTube channel. I find them particularly sensitive in clearing not only earthbound spirit but also everyday people and their homes that contain attachments or entities.

When working with a client, I see the inside of the chakras as for me it is a tool to gather information about what she or he is truly ready to release and heal from. The inside of a chakra to me, looks like a wide, round room often with a fire pit in the very centre. The fire pit is used to release the overcrowded energy within a power spot. I will experience the hoarding of objects in these rooms, with overflowing trash cans, dusty curtains drawn shut over windows of possibility and filing cabinets full to the brim with reasons why a client should not love too openly, trust her own self-worth, let go of a toxic relationship or even progress in her life.

Ideally, what we all want is to own magnetically clear and shiny energy centres that feel in balance, easily attract what we desire and resonate with new love and power. Sounds great! But…you are already aware that before beginnings must be the endings. Everyone you know has some decluttering work to do, some of which can take a lifetime – so you may as well start!

Your readiness comes with stepping towards fear. You may already know that you have had enough of the old ways … the old sense of low worth. The fact that you are reading this book may also be a sign of your new commitment to being a light for yourself and others.

With courageous commitment must come a new relationship with patience. Impatience will pull you backwards and comes from ego, not from soul.

Slowdown in your waking life, become more present and pace yourself. Learn to work in short bursts of energy and spend the rest of your time energetically relaxing in order to receive. This journey of yours will not be complete at your death. We are like onions – just when we think we are done, we find another, deeper layer of evolutionary opportunity.

So, get to know your chakras. Develop a sense of your body becoming a barometer for energy body, then notice which chakra draws your attention and feels in need of your healing focus. Read books about the work done in this area from more experienced practitioners. Two favourites of mine are 'Chakras and their Archetypes' by Ambika Wauters and 'Opening to Spirit' by Caroline Shola Arewa - both publications wonderfully deep and inspirational.

Develop methods to rebalance you, particularly in times of stress. Firstly, practice getting out of the head. The busyness of the mind can keep us in the fear and worry of the past or the future, especially if we have not disciplined our mindset sufficiently.

Take the time to make time to stay grounded in your body as this is where your energy lives.

One simple grounding technique is to imagine that within the centre of your belly is a calm, clear lake, deep and beautiful, the surface of the water so clear you can see the brightly coloured fish darting in and amongst the smooth rocks on the bottom of the lake bed. Now bring in the other senses, hearing the sound of water lapping at the banks of the lake, feeling a warm gentle breeze against the side of your cheek and the texture of the grass beneath your feet. Feel the sunlight above you set within a blue sky. As you breathe, allow all this warm golden light of the sun to draw down and into the top of your head through the crown chakra, lightening your energy and expanding your sense of peace so that with every exhalation anything unnecessary can be expelled easily.

Breathe this wonderful sense of radiance down through the central channel of your body, imagining it illuminating every cell, every bone, every muscle and every energetic layer view, through the spine and the pelvis and all the way down beyond the sole of your feet into the ground. Planting yourself ankle-deep in the earth at all times is a very powerful way to stay grounded, safer and stronger.

And because you live in the modern world, the other crucial part of your intuitive development is protection. There are many ways to insulate your energy, from the outside muddy energy such as surrounding yourself with golden balls, pink bubbles, purple flames, cocoons of white light and so on. My personal favourite is the disco ball, but you will need to into it what suits you best and works for your current state of evolution.

On a personal growth note, neutrality and non-resistance are other forms of psychic protection. As you grow stronger in your light, there will be an opposing force that will often try to challenge your increase in power. An example of this might be that you hear negative gossip about you or that someone feels an injustice has been done and is blaming you, despite you being innocent of the charge.

The trick here, if you want to continue getting stronger in light, is to not react. This can be enormously difficult for humans as we are quick to war and sometimes slower to reflection. Consider this merely a test from your support team of guides and higher self and continue raising your vibrations upwards rather than getting caught in the pull from down below.

The ego can remain a dominant force in the lives of many spiritual practitioners, but my advice is not to become one of them. You just need enough ego to maintain healthy boundaries, to say 'do not treat me like that' to someone who needs to hear that. That is all the ego you need. Any more, and you will imbalance your spiritual development. Your work will be diluted, the energy less powerful - all because you need to be the famous or visible one, rather than the purpose that is attempting to channel its way through you.

Holding a strong memory of you being 'One with All' maintains a natural humility that allows more power to come through you. Seeing yourself as equal to all souls in this 'schoolyard of life' will equip you with far more shamanic skills than any of those who compare themselves to others, in either superior or inferior ways.

You are like everybody else on the planet: merely an instrument for energy to pass through and be directed, upon your choice - towards light or dark.

Choose to be a spiritual leader in your family, however, by role modelling what intuition, gratitude, joy and loving acceptance looks and feels like. Own your shadow without blame, learn how to clear intensity with the clarity and honesty of a four-year-old child and remembering that have chosen your family and partner to heal original wounds.

When you are committed to seeing the light in others, their souls expand.

When you are committed to acknowledging the light in yourself, you can only go upwards.

11

CLEARING YOUR HOME

Just like our physical bodies, most people are unaware that they may be living in a house that is also hoarding energy.

The best time to clear your personal space is obviously before you move in, when you can walk around each empty room, reactivate the healthy energy, call upon the guardian spirits of the house to align with your energy, discover what trees and animal spirits protect the property and get rid of the heavier, harmful energies and entities that have lived there for years.

However, as this is not always possible, you can spring-clean your space today, energetically-speaking and make today the first day of your new home energy instead!

There are methodical steps to cleansing your own space.

The first one is to choose a time when you can be alone in it, and can do this process uninterrupted by neighbours, friends or the telephone.

The next thing you need to do is book in your intention to

cleanse, with your guides. Even if you do not have a relationship with them, simply by acknowledging their presence with gratitude, accelerates the power of your clearing process.

Thank them for being around you in your life. They are trying to help and guide you, regardless of whether you listen or take the time to notice all the little gifts and miracles that your energy is aligned with in everyday living.

Tell them that you will be clearing your home of all harmful energy and entities, give them the day and time you'll be doing it and ask them for their protection and assistance in directing these harmful energies easily towards the Light. Then thank them in advance for being there.

Let's go vortex-hunting!

This planet is covered by a 'leyline' grid of energy that highlights power spots all over the earth – such as The Great Pyramid, Jerusalem and Gulaga, the Mother of Uluru in Australia. On Google, you will find a map pinpointing all the major vortices across the world. I find it inaccurate and simplistic, so do not take that research as gospel. It is interesting to notice that all the early Christian churches were built along the leylines, particularly in the UK. The energy is at its most powerful at the vortex – and can be used for either light or dark.

Where two leylines meet is a point that we call a 'vortex', a centre of energetic power. Like your chakras, these are the Earth's. You'll find many of these vortices in your home, sometimes one or two in every room. They are such great energy, you may as well switch them on!

First, however, use them as a vacuum to suck and remove anything that is *not* of light.

The next thing is to make your own pair of dowsers, or practice using a pendulum. This is a handy tool that will help you find exactly where the harmful energies will be in your home. A dowser or a pendulum will help you locate the leyline 'good' energy in your home.

Then, go outside the house into a sunny place which feels loving, close your eyes, and protect yourself with white light, and call upon your guides. Then, re-enter your home with a clear intention to look for vortexes.

Just as your home is criss-crossed with good leylines, there are also negative energy lines. These are lines containing negative ions, radium and electro-magnetic energy. Whilst you cannot remove negative lines, you can at least direct them into the structure of the building rather than have them influencing the spaces and human occupants in every room.

Back to the good energy. What does a vortex look like? For me, it's a tornado or spiral of light. This will be the image my dowser or pendulum detect.

Learning how to use a dowser or a pendulum can be very easy. First, get two wire coat hangers and cut them at two points with a pair of wire cutters. Make one cut below the hook on the left. Then, make another cut in the right-hand corner.

To clearly see what my dowsers look like, please look at the dowsing classes on my *pastorlucybaker* YouTube channel, as I mentioned before. Of course, you can buy ready-made dowsers, but I prefer to make and program my own.

Then bend them until they are each L-shaped and your dowsers are ready for programming. Now, hold them with your index finger and thumb just below the L-curve with the shorter part of the 'L' beneath your fingers and the longest part facing out in front of you, parallel to the ground and close together. Then close your eyes, and visualize the word 'YES' – and, while saying this word out loud several times, manually turn the dowsers outwards so that they look wide open. You have just programmed your dowsers to find something, as that will be the position the rods will move to, when you locate the vortex in a room.

Now, program in the word 'NO' – visualizing the word, and saying out loud several times, whilst manually moving the rods towards each other so that they cross over. Now you have programmed your dowsers to confirm the absence of harmful energy when you have successfully cleansed your space!

The strength of dowsing lies in your power of visualisation. Just as you throw a ball ahead of a dog to catch, so you need to throw a clear and specific image of what you are seeking to find head of your dowsing. The stronger you can see, feel or taste the object you are trying to find the more success you will have.

Now, you need to practice. Practice getting a good, clear visual in your head of a few objects, then deliberately place them in visible sight and walk slowly towards the object with your dowsers, and wait to see if your dowsers turn by themselves, into the YES position, when you stand over the object. If they don't – you either have to reprogramme, this time more clearly, or visualize the object more strongly. Go, on, try this exercise with a selection of objects, like chocolate, car keys, a crystal, money, a book.

Once you can dowse, you can find your vortexes. Out loud, say 'I wish to locate the presence of a leyline vortex of white light'. Then, imagine the two blazing light lines of energy meeting in an X, and start walking around the room.

When your dowsers respond, you can either place a rose quartz (which is always a great cleanser and balancer) on the vortex or stand closely to it, facing the vortex and take a deep breath.

Remember! Strength of visualization and a clear intention is your focus. The better these two ingredients are, the more powerful your cleansing will be. As you stand near the vortex, your focus is magnified, so make the most of it.

Now as you visualize a shaft of brilliant white light – so bright it could make your eyes water – shooting straight up out of the vortex and moving around the room, into every nook and cranny, under every cupboard, inside every light-fitting, around each corner, peeling off any harmful, heavy and dull energy with its intensity, sucking it up and sending it upwards through the ceiling like a furious vacuum cleaner – say these words:

'I focus and amplify the life force energy of the planet to move up and through this vortex and remove all harmful energies and entities and DIRECT them towards the Light for further growth and healing! There is no further growth and healing available to you on this level – go now towards the Light, as I now claim this space in the name of …. (add your own words here, such as Light, love, abundance, health and harmony) in the name of (again, add your favourite deity, guides, religious masters).

At this time, I also forcefully exhale as when I stand on a vortex I become the channel through which energy can move in or out.

Often, I will feel my heart chakra vibrate when I know a room has been forcefully cleansed. Now you open the windows, light a white candle, place it on a surface in this newly cleansed room and say a prayer in the form of a blessing, calling out to the angels and guides from the Light to protect and charge this room with love and protection, and that only that which is of your highest good may enter here.

Now you have an empty room, if you have done a good job. It's a 'good' empty feeling, not a lonely one – and the space that you've just cleared can now be filled with good, healthy, happy new affirmations, actions, attitudes and energy.

Repeat this process with each room, and then do the outside – front and back. This is the simplest technique of vortex energy work, and one of the most effective. I have had Feng Shui masters ask me to cleanse their space, as this work is one of the most powerful on the planet. Treat vortex energy with respect and it will reward you greatly.

12

CLEARING YOUR WORKPLACE

Of course, now you know how to clear your home – you can apply the same technique to your workplace, especially if you have your own business. For others, however, creeping around with dowsers when everyone else has gone home or do a vortex ritual under the curious eye of a surveillance camera might not a good idea!

One alternative way, made even more potent if you can visualize well, is to draw an aerial picture or floorplan of your workplace. Place this on a vortex at home and imagine you are walking from room to room, seeing images and furniture clearly and speaking your releasement words.

There are also additional ways you can cleanse your space at work – from placing a small vase of water on your desk and having a cleansed crystal out of sight, to ancient method gathered from global wisdom.

Some Native Americans use a simple prayer technique to ward off darker energies - by holding up their hands, palms facing upwards and breathing deeply. The Tibetans move from room to room with incense and song - singing loudly, beating a drum or a cymbal or simply clapping - to remove stale energy.

Feng Shui is another philosophy that has gained tremendous popularity in the west over the last two decades. In brief, there are nine areas of life that correspond to your environment. By clearing out your clutter in the workplace you are restoring your career path to clarity and ensuring greater protection in doing so. Sort through old files, toss out all that documentation you may no longer need, give your desk a polish, add fresh flowers, fix the squeak in that office chair and saturate your workplace with brilliant white light - so light it could almost make your eyes water!

When your life flows well, it's often because your lifeforce energy feels healthy and upbeat. Anytime you hoard or hold on to old, heavy energy, you'll magnetise resonating vibes back towards you. Often, they can present as attachments and generalized blocked energy – so decide today to start shifting the old.

Space-clearing will open your energy flow and remember – just as the famous *ying-yang* symbol shows us with its curling black and white image – as above, so below, as outer, so inner. In other words, how clear and cleansed you are on the inside will be reflected by how your outside environment looks – at home and at work.

As the Buddhists say, 'nothing is permanent'. Our job as humans is to learn from pain but release the suffering. To not hold on to any experience, no matter how difficult. Instead, to value whatever lessons are being offered to and release any unnecessary energy to the Light.

If you work in a stressful or unpleasant environment, it's also good to focus some time on creating a 'force field' of protection around you – as if you are insulated in a mirror-ball or crystal bubble, shielded from anything that is not of your highest good. Do this in addition to saturating the entire workplace with light.

When I work within a new space, I perform several rituals. As I move from room to room, I imagine myself a bright light moving into darkness, filling each corner, each nook, each cranny with powerful white and yellow light.

I then place sacred objects underneath, inside and on top of my work space, ideally out of sight of all others. These could be crystals, rocks and other gifts from the Universe that have been imprinted with power and magic by my prayer and intention. Before placing them, they should also have been thoroughly cleansed to ensure that they are clean, willing sponges waiting to absorb any energy in their new habitat – either by placing in saltwater under the light of a full moon, buried in earth for three days, placed on a vortex or cleansed through strong visualisation.

In silence, I will then search out the heart of the work space by visualising the strongest spiral of light flowing up from the ground beneath the foundations of the building. I can do this with my dowsing rods, pendulum or my hands, asking for assistance in locating the pink or green pulsating energy of the centre of this Universe.

Once found, I will stand or sit within it, sending and receiving its blessing, and strengthening the energy of love, healing and protection that I wish to emanate from this space. I will always cleanse the space with prayer, shamanic words and special rituals.

If you are unsure, remember that your intention holds the power. Follow your heart and trust that you will say the words and do the ritual that is perfect for you!

At this point, your workplace cleanse is complete, save from the humans that work within it. If the workplace is set within nature or near to shrubs, flowers or trees, I would also ask for their cooperation and assistance, introducing myself to the Nature Spirits, especially the guardians of the building - the trees, who see all and know all. I connect with them by touching their trunks and asking them who they are and what is their purpose, and allow a space within my intuition to receive their answer. With humility, I thank them and ask for their protection and blessing.

If you like, you can also extend your cleansing to direction blessings – and this is great to do at home especially. As I move around the rim of a house or workplace building, I carry a compass and as I reach the four directions, I stop and say a prayer to the north, south, east and west. At each man-made corner of the building, I also ask for angelic guidance and watchfulness.

When I lived in an old house in California years ago, it was a gift to witness four angels (one at each corner) stand and listen, the tips of their wings touching my new roof. They were larger than I had imagined and completed a very powerful house-cleansing and blessing ritual for me that day.

Finally, I sit outside and imagine myself a bird, looking down on an aerial plan of my property. I begin to trace a line around the perimeters, moving clockwise or anti clockwise. As it's difficult for most of us to concentrate upon an unbroken line for long, you may have to go over a section a few times until you are satisfied that you have a clear, strong line stretching around your workplace or house and garden.

Thus completed, I then fill this line with white energy - powerful, thick, cleansing white energy - and as bright as a naked light bulb. I always visualize this energy as thick and almost opaque - and often use an image from the first 'Superman' movie.

We've all seen 'Superman', the movie, right? Well, remember when the young Superman visits the ice castle, and meets with the spirit of his father? Those stalagmites of ice were thick, and when Superman passed them, all the detail we could see was the colour of his clothing. So that is the thickness I imagine, too. Gold or pink is also wonderful, and again, follow your own intuition.

I then begin to build this line upwards, until the line now resembles a white, energetic wall around my property. I continue to build it up and up until I join all four corners over the roof, perhaps 10 feet or so above the top of my workplace or house, in a dome shape. Now I have a dome of white energy, encasing my entire space within power and protection.

I like to add one further gift. As I leave my dome each day, I like to switch it on so that it emits a loud hum, like an electrical force, repelling all those who enter my space with harmful intent. My whole family also loves to complete the ritual by singing as we leave our property, 'Bye house with lots of white energy!'

Said each day, and the dome rebuilt each week, you will notice the benefits. Do your cleansing in your work environment and you will find the energy shifts there also.

13

OTHER WAYS TO BREAK CURSES

Throughout all cultures, there are ways to jinx and ways to break jinxes or curses. My all-time favourite used to be a visit to a Romany man who lived in the south west area of England, close to the border of Cornwall, where there is strong Celtic energy.

In this place, the home of my ancestors, I would watch him break jinxes for people by placing his hand on the head of the person and saying a certain phrase in his Gypsy tongue, ending with a sudden shake of his body. Lovely to watch, and it appeared to work well.

With everything, whatever you do with intention, will work.

There are shamanic ways to lift curses, although many of these are hidden away from those who are not shaman. What I can tell you is that the shamanic ways I use are similar to soul retrieval work I have done – going back in time to draw into the present moment that part of a person's soul that has been frozen in time by an event.

There is a plethora of herbal, and witchy ways to work on lifting curses.

One example is to run a bath during the new to full moon cycle, and fill it with elderberries, orange flowers and gentian. Climb into your bath, and begin to cover your body with this water, and as you do so, say:

'I call upon Luna, Goddess of Women and the Moon to remove and direct all that is not for my highest good, all that is not of Light upwards and beyond.' Then, as you dry yourself, visualize your energy saturated with light, with any heavy energy seeping off you like steam. Finish your ritual with an appreciation for your guides and for Luna herself – and say, 'blessed be'.

The more you can repeat any ritual, the stronger it becomes.

You could do this each night from the new moon if you so desire – or in the case of one client, on every Monday night – which is a great spell-casting night for women.

Another method is to write the symptoms of your 'curse' down on paper, emptying it out of your body. Write whatever words come out and trust your first impressions. Then, light a candle and step outside as late at night as possible, under the light of the waning moon, which symbolises release.

Focus on the energy you are wanting to clear then set fire to your paper, burning it safely outside, and imagining the fire cleansing your energy as it does so. The waning of the moon – from full moon to dark moon - is the best time in its cycle for removing curse energy.

Add your own words – such as 'from this moment, I refuse to do struggle, poverty or penetrability of another's energy that does not serve me. From this moment, I am open to attracting forces of light, harmlessness and love into my life only. So, mote it be!'

Then allow the candle to burn itself out of its own accord before burying the stump and ashes of your paper into a small hole dug in your garden. Close it over with a prayer.

Two of the most powerful ways to break curses is within group energy, and creating your own words within a spell.

Group energy sets up karma and releases it, which is why you want to make sure that, whatever group of people you are drawn to, the intent of the group is for the good of all. If you feel at all uneasy upon entering a new group, then leave immediately. Once you relax into such an energy, it will become easier for your energy to be vulnerable to attack.

There are covens of white and dark witches, and groups of dark and white energy that occur nightly all over the planet. Use your energy with integrity and your contribution within that group will bear fruit. Use it for dark intent and you will face the repercussions for lifetimes!

I used to run prosperity classes, with a group of interested people attending once a week for six weeks. Within that timeframe, all but one person received their focus – for one person, it was a highly paying job, for another a dream house, and another a gorgeous partner. Group energy is a powerful tool and is to be used with respect.

One word of caution that I need to add here, is about the current craze about Halloween. In the USA, this is, after Christmas, the most celebrated holiday of the year.

What less conscious folk don't realize is that *whatever we focus on, grows.* On this night, the focus is on dark energy, regardless of its disguise of harmless fun. It is group energy.

I once lived close to Dartmoor, which, in the UK, is a mecca for black witchcraft – and without fail, a few days before Halloween, all the cats used to disappear, especially the black ones. They still do, year after year.

What happens is that a 'portal' or doorway that leads to other worlds is created by our focus each year during this time, and with any portal, it can not only release energy, but attract it. For many years, I would go into the forest on Halloween night with my faithful moon ritual dog, Diana, sit down on a tree stump and move into a deep meditation.

Almost immediately, I would get a sense of being joined by a huge global circle of other shaman, intuitives and healers from across the planet. In this space, we would focus and soon discover that our purpose in coming together was to maintain the boundaries of the positive leylines surrounding the earth.

One year, I knew with certainty that a dark group in Egypt was attempting to use the open portal of the Halloween focus to break down a leyline. We succeeded. Light, especially in strong group energy, is always stronger. That night, as I left the forest, there was an air of spiritual celebration in the air.

Maybe choose a new ritual next Halloween. Add your harmless, loving and potent energy to a group of lightworkers near you, instead of joining in the traditional play. You might enjoy it even more!

And as for writing your own spells – yes, you can do it. There is nothing sacred about using somebody else's, especially if yours are more thoughtful, created just for your circumstances and containing your own intensity of focus.

Other ways to break curses include gathering herbs, creating paper talismans and tracing the ancestral energy of the curser. In one such case that I heard about, the curse energy turned out to be of Portuguese nationality, and called for a specific technique. In Portuguese culture, the man is a god and the woman, considered to be of less worthy energy. However, in the spirit world and after death, matriarchy rules in this country with the female spirits becoming dominant in their energy.

It is often to these spirits – called 'The Angry Mothers' – that curse-lifters ask for help. Sometimes they may visit the curse-lifting ritual as dark birds. Other rituals may include bathing in herbs such as basil or salt, using holy water and water taken from sacred circles.

I trained as a medium in Africa for 12 years and often attended 'sangoma' or witchdoctor rituals where I had the honour of witnessing energy at its most intense. Bones were thrown, dancers became hypnotized, energy moved in swirling colours, and prayers were called out. I have also seen wise women from eastern Europe use beans as a way of countering bad energy.

If you're curious, explore the diversity of methods. Google, delve through old books in antique shops, explore the mysteries of history or find someone who works in shamanic ways to receive a direct experience from.

Magic is such a boundless and exciting field!

14

CREATING IMPENETRABILITY

Impenetrability goes far beyond psychic protection.

The ability to maintain a strong, loving and harmless force field that keeps us safe through challenge and turmoil must start with a decision to be honest about who we are and commit to travelling deeply into our most innermost, darkest corners and into places and memories that our fears would have us not recall.

It's at those moments in life, when we feel we cannot go on, cannot live with the pain of reality that we are in most need of a change of perspective that could reactivate our protection: what if we are merely at a turning point, rather than at an end?

Think about it. How quickly you or I imagine that each dose of painful difficulty, each insurmountable obstacle is the end, the final straw - that we have failed, it's over, we might as well give up, forget it, escape from it, turn away from it, reject it and separate from loved ones over it.

How conclusive we are! All those souls watching us from the spirit plane must be falling over themselves in their laughter, with their clearer view of our entire life flight plan! Ah well, maybe we also stood up there and chuckled at other humans, too!

Peter Rengel, a facilitator of the California-based Human Awareness Institute workshops suggests that if we don't feel the fear, we are not growing.

We've all, I guess, been at 'comfortable' points in our lives, when it's easier to 'put up' with circumstances and people, than it is to change it. What keeps us there is our limiting belief that there may be no better quality of life, that this could be all there is, all we deserve.

But, consider this - what if your doorbell rang one day, and there stood a millionaire on the doorstep, with a large check with your name on.

'Here,' he or she says. 'This is for you to go out and create a whole new life with. I have a list of perfect partners for you in my limo, the best nanny in the Universe to care for your children while you are busy recreating your life, and of course, money is no object.'

Well, I can wager that most of us, once we had checked out the authenticity of the offer, would be off in a matter of seconds. We now had proof of a 'better life' and we were going to grab it. No longer would we settle for second-best!

Well, the lesson of Spiritual Awareness, is that you have all this being offered to you now, only you are not aware of it.

You cannot see it, or have it handed to you on a platter - but, with a little work, healing, conscious discipline, and the belief that you alone can create a whole new reality -this new life is yours. It's waiting in the wings for you to catch up. Some of us, because of our disbelief or distrust, will not reach this prize this lifetime. But others will.

Trust in the Universe - it's much more than you can see. And, consider the possibility that whoever suggested to you a very long time ago, that you would not always get what you want - could have been disastrously wrong.

Many of us have grown up with these family affirmations, spoon-fed to us by unaware parents who were, in turn, fed these from their own experiences or decisions in their lives, and by their parents:

- *You don't always get what you want*
- *Nobody's perfect*
- *You have to work hard for the money*
- *Life is hard*
- *You only live once*
- *You've got to grab what you can in life*
- *Maybe this is all there is*
- *Don't get too big for your boots*
- *There are no second chances*

And so on - makes life a little sad and rather limited, don't you think? Is this how the children of the universal life force should live? Is this all we are, all we can expect?

Once, however, we understand that these little titbits are merely free samples of larger karmic tests, we can learn how to simply hop over them, or refuse to include them in our vocabularies anymore – especially words like 'should' or 'must' that tend to be connected to shame, guilt or duty.

The more we continue to trust our intuition, and commit to continuous growth while we are living our lives, no matter how dark or frightening growth can feel, the more we clear a space for more powerful and protective energy to enter our lives.

The deeper we travel into ourselves, the more painful it will become, initially. If we know this from the outset, it can give us the strength we need to continue the journey.

It is as if we are diving into a bottomless pool, and as we stand at the water's edge, our toes curling over the side of its banks, we notice the surface is almost solid, with murky, dense crust -as if no-one has ever broken through this top layer in centuries.

At this point, it's a lot easier to step back, and consider a safer place to go for a little swim. Your conscious mind begins to seize control, and suggests that you don't really need to do this - why on earth would you put yourself through all that muck?

However, this is where your Higher Self, your intuition, some inner need you have that comes from a deeper place that any part of your consciousness, whispers to you – 'if your life is not happy, if you yearn to feel empowered, confident, aware, then be brave and dive! If you have a feeling that there's more to life than what you have, then dive - and trust in the support of the Universe. Know that you are always in the right place at the right time.'

So, you jump - but only if you are ready to do this 100 per cent!

At first the feelings of isolation and discomfort are huge, as you battle for breath, fighting your way through the wet darkness, until you feel a hand reaching out to guide you onwards.

You trust it and allow yourself to be guided - or you reject it fearfully, not wanting to be seen as vulnerable or needy - and battle on stoically, often for a lot longer than your journey would have been, had you learned the lesson of Trust.

Perhaps, the second time around, when you feel the hand again - and begin to understand that your decision to reject first has not cost you rejection in return - you may accept the support and move into a place of knowing.

To show vulnerability is a sign of power, inner strength and potency - and not the man-made definition of weakness that comes from ancient patriarchal fears. To feel all your emotions is to know yourself.

And, to move forward, sometimes, we must go back in time.

In addition to your spiritual development, it's very important to also focus on your personal development. By this I mean that you hold to the intention to move away from the trauma of your past to a place where you can accept the journey of your soul, view the most difficult people in your life as teachers who taught you how to install healthier boundaries and walk away from toxic relationships and finally arrive at a place where you can celebrate your history.

Investigate therapists in your area or online. Learn how to trust other, more experienced facilitators to help draw out of you that which you will continue to hold if you try to do all of this on your own. There are countless powerful and loving workshops around the world that can help you change your life script and your perspective. If you hold the intention to be a light in the middle of this dark Earth plane, you will need to identify and then release any shame, guilt, self-criticism or unworthiness you have been carrying.

Develop trust in yourself. Learn to trust your ability to make wise choices. When you trust your intuition and your souls knowing, you will be facing the right way.

Give yourself permission to become authentic, without the masks humans wear each day. Explore your entire, colourful palette of emotions, and not merely the ones that were deemed appropriate to feel in your family of origin.

All of us carry a masculine and feminine energy within us, regardless of physical gender or sexual orientation. Our job is to become balanced and accepting of both, healing the old ways of expressing the emotions from each and releasing the need for control.

Above all, love and appreciate who you have become. It is only when you look back that you realise how far you have come. Celebrate your progress.

Of course, there is always more to do, more to heal. The fact that you are in a human body as a spiritual being indicates that there is a need for you to be here in school. Decide to not place other people above or below you. Each human being has his or her shadow and light within. Nelson Mandela, the Dalai Lama, Mother Teresa - no human being is above you. Some may be more experienced in some skills than you are, but you are also more experienced in other skills than they are.

This is the beginning of developing a strong and healthy self-esteem. A daily practice I always encourage my students to do, is to verbally give themselves two minutes of self-appreciation in the mirror each day - not for what they do, but for who they are. Do your inner child work. Inside of you, is a small scared part that never grows up - a part that often have holds on to the most intense of emotions and painful experiences in your life.

For as long as you focus outwards caring for others more than you care and nurture yourself your path ahead will not be as rewarding or progressive as it could be. If you have learnt how to be your harshest critic, then inner child work is your top priority. Visit my website at lucybaker.net and download one of the most significant hypnotherapy journeys you could do which connects you to you and evicts the inner critic from your energy. As the late Stan Dale of the Human Awareness Institute used to say, 'if God wanted to hide on this earth, he would hide inside a human being, as that's the last place we would think of looking…'

So, it is time to love yourself more fully. The part of you that is soul needs your self-acceptance. And, think of the greater impact this new relationship within would have on the outside world! Your healing ripples out within the collective consciousness in a way that you will never know.

As always you have a choice. Everything we do is either an act of love or a cry for love, often expressed as victim or with violence.

Tremendous healing takes place at this tender level, and it's a place that you can only reach with a willingness to grow and to feel some pain, before you can feel a deeper level of joy than you have ever known. You are then able to shed your old, painful skin for a glowing, rich, healthy, aware and happy one.

Magically, you'll began to attract other powerful people into your life, until your world will look vastly different from a decade ago. You'll choose not to isolate yourself out of fear.

You'll understand that to receive love, you first have to give it - what you put out, comes back, remember?

And, the first person you must learn to give love to, is yourself. The rest is easy.

This is the key to real curse-lifting and future impenetrability!

ABOUT THE AUTHOR

Well respected in her field of psycho-spirituality, Lucy Baker helps people retrieve power, call back their spirit and get out of their way, using her unique blend of spirituality, shamanism and self-development. A natural child rescue medium, Lucy has worked as a Bridge between light and dark since 1972, both within living people and discarnate Spirit.

Recognised as shaman by a gathering of the Indigenous in 1996 following a 24-year apprenticeship, Lucy's clients include Aboriginal people who need to remove curses, ambassadors who need to attract more charisma, police officers and nurses who require greater protection and everyday people who want to gain their ideal weight, health, relationship and career success.

Considered the go-to Spiritual Counsellor for thousands of evolving women and men, Lucy is a Medicine Teacher with over 30 years of teaching experience. In 2005, she was awarded the Psychic of the Year in Australia, 2005. In 2006, she was a Facilitator alongside Dolores Cannon and Dr Sunny Satin at the World Congress of Regression Therapists in Delhi and remains a popular speaker at various international medical groups and theosophical societies.

Lucy is also the author of the popular Instagram and Facebook 'The Lucy Daily', an inspirational free message that enjoys over 20K readers a week.

To join her workshops, download a powerful hypno-journey or book a private online session, visit lucybaker.net

"In the darkest of darkness,

there is always a pinpoint of Light."

— Lucy Baker

Printed in Great
Britain
by Amazon